Colonial Fireplace Cooking & Early American Recipes

Margaret Taylor Chalmers

Illustrations by Margaret McAlister
Cover by Phillip Knapman

eberly press

1004 Michigan Ave.

East Lansing, MI 48823

Copyright 1979, 1995 by **eberly press** ™

Library of Congress Catalog Card No. 76-66274

ISBN 0-932296-04-1

Early American Saltbox Home in Greenfield Village

GROWING UP BY THE IRISH FIRESIDE

Fireplaces in our new modern homes today are much more ornamental than functional. There is no comparison between a 16th century fireplace that was built for two basic functions–heating the home and cooking the family meals–and the fireplace built in our dens and family rooms to give the feeling of warmth and coziness on cold winter nights.

However, an interesting phenomenon is taking place in the American home over the past few years. Women and men are interested in having their fireplaces become more functional in the area of cooking. I know because of the enormous growth of my fireplace cooking classes in the last few years at the colonial kitchen of Clinton Inn at Greenfield Village in Dearborn, Michigan.

It is with much pleasure I greet this new interest in fireplace cooking because I well remember the many wonderful times I spent in our large kitchen in Portglenone County Antirm, Ireland waiting with eager anticipation for the first batch of treacle scones to come off the griddle of the peat fueled fireplace or the first loaf of soda bread to come out of the Dutch oven.

There is nothing to compare with the rich smell of burning wood or peat intermingled with the fragrant odor of fresh breads and stews being cooked over an open fire. Even now I can still fell the warmth, love and caring that surrounded me in that kitchen long ago.

Bread and scones were usually made in large quantities two days a week, and I was always told they could not be eaten until dinner or supper. However, inevitably as my grandmother would lift the first batch from the griddle in her snowy white apron, one hot fragrant scone would drop to the hearth and she would turn to me with a twinkle in her eye and say, "Well, Margaret, that scone won't be fit for the table." That was all I needed to hear as I scurried to the hearth, retrieved the fallen scone, dusted off the ashes and ran to the creamery to spread it with fresh churned butter. It was, of course, devoured with relish.

Unfortunately, today's children will never experience many of these pleasures. However, with a modern fireplace, a minimum investment in some good black iron pots and simple recipes, similar scenes could be created on a cold, snowy Sunday afternoon.

–MTC, 1979

Table of Contents

General Directions for Fireplace Cooking...8
Fireplace Utensils...8
Cooking Utensils...9
Care of Black Iron Pots..9
Methods of Cooking..10

FIREPLACE MENUS & RECIPES

Fireplace I...14
Fireplace II...22
Fireplace III..27

EARLY AMERICAN MENUS & RECIPES

Victorian...33
Plantation...42
Creole...50
Northwestern..57
Irish..64
Pennsylvania Dutch I..71
Pennsylvania Dutch II...77
Smoky Mountain...85

GENERAL DIRECTIONS FOR FIREPLACE COOKING

Obviously, the most important item to prepare is a good fire, using a variety of hardwoods that will give a good bed of warm red coals which is essential to good cooking. Both the amount of coals used and the heat produced will determine the temperature. Don't be frightened off by this experience because there is no automatic temperature control. Just relax, have fun and follow these simple directions.

One important note. Fire can burn people and homes as well as food. So treat it with respect. Use plain common sense to avoid accidents.

Fireplace Utensils

Andirons were used in early colonial fireplaces to elevate and lay the logs on. If you are fortunate enough to own a pair of andirons these can be used in the same way today. However, if you are like most people you will probably have to settle for a modern day fireplace basket which does the job equally as well.

I suggest you select one that is strong enough to support sturdy legs and that has fairly large open grill-work that will enable hot coals to fall through onto the hearth.

To move the coals under the various cooking pots, a long handled shovel, scoop or spade is essential. Tongs are also an important instrument for shifting and arranging logs to keep them burning properly. NEVER try to lift the cooking pots with the tongs as this could be very dangerous.

Cooking Utensils

Black cast iron pots are almost a must in my opinion for fireplace cooking. However, other heavy duty pots can be used, but be prepared for a lot of cleaning as they will be blackened when the meal is finished cooking.

The vessels, in most cases, have to be elevated above the hearth so the coals can be shoveled underneath.

Colonial cooks used long-handled iron ladles and spoons. These, however, are very fast conductors of heat. Therefore, the handles become very hot very quickly. For this reason I choose not to use metal cooking utensils, but, like my mother and grandmother, love the feel of a well used wooden spoon in the palm of my hand. I always keep a whole crock full of various lengths and sizes of wooden spoons within easy reach of both stove and fireplace.

Care of Black Iron Pots

Like all fine heirlooms, iron pots need and deserve a little extra care. Given this, they will serve well through several life times.

If your pots are already seasoned, they should be washed after each use with a mild detergent. If any food has stuck to the pot, coarse salt should be rubbed over hardened particles of food until the pot comes clean - NEVER use any other abrasives. Pots should then be thoroughly dried. Rub vegetable oil sparingly over all surfaces of pots and lids, both inside and out, then let stand for a few minutes. Wipe with a paper towel to remove all surplus oil. If this simple procedure is followed faithfully your black iron pots will always serve you well and be a pleasure to use.

If new cast-iron pots are going to be purchased, care should be taken to ensure pot surfaces are of the proper smooth texture without porous pits or roughness.

New pots can be seasoned by rubbing all surfaces with vegetable oil or as our colonial forefathers, or should I say foremothers, did by rubbing all surfaces with salt pork. The pots should then be placed in a 200 degree oven for several hours. This may have to be repeated several times in order for the pots to gain that patina that comes from constant use and proper care.

Iron pots should not be confined to fireplace cooking alone. Personally, I never use any other cookware whether I am cooking on a 16th century fireplace, over a camp fire or on top of my 20th century electric range.

Methods of Cooking

Fireplaces built for the function of cooking were always equipped with a crane or swinging arm. These canes were usually fitted with a combination of chains and fire hooks which were used to suspend pots at various heights in order to somewhat regulate the degree of heat required for whatever cooking was being done. This of course is the ideal instrument to use and if you are fortunate enough to have one in your fireplace you are well prepared to produce a succulent meal right from your hearth.

Other items needed are:

Cast iron trivets with legs 3-4 inches high that pots may be set on and the coals placed underneath.

Two bricks set on the hearth with a heavy grate laid across them. Barbecue grills, oven or old refrigerator racks are usually strong enough to do a good job of this. Extreme caution must be used if this is the method chosen as these make-shift grills may be easily tipped over if not handled with care.

Spider Dutch ovens - stew pots and/or fry pans and griddles. (These are pots with the legs already attached).

Two bricks set on the hearth with a heavy grate laid across them. Barbecue grills, oven or old refrigerator racks are usually strong enough to do a good job of this. Extreme caution must be used if this is the method chosen as these make-shift grills may be easily tipped over if not handled with care.

Iron Pots and Trammel on Crane

Fireplace
Recipes

FIREPLACE I

Burgoo
Irish Soda Bread
Citrus Rind Marmalade
Cloth Pudding
Hot Lemon and Vanilla Sauce
Fresh Churned Butter
Mulled Wine

BURGOO

6 Tbl. bacon drippings
1 lb. shoulder of veal
2 roasting chickens
4 qts. water
1 Tbl. salt
4 onions
2 cloves garlic, crushed
8 potatoes, diced
6 stalks celery with leaves
8 tomatoes, quartered
6 carrots
2-3 fresh green peppers
2 c. fresh lima beans

1/4 tsp. crushed red pepper
4 cloves
Bay leaf
1 tsp. fresh thyme
3 Tbl. brown sugar
1/2 tsp. black pepper
*2 c. okra slices
*6 c. fresh corn (cut from cob)
*1/2 c. butter
*1 c. flour
*1 c. chopped parsley
Shredded cabbage

Heat half the fat in a large kettle. Add veal and brown well. Add chickens, water and salt. Cover and cook until tender. Remove meat and chickens. Set aside until cool. Break into small pieces. Discard fat and bones. Return meat to broth in kettle.

Add all other ingredients except those with an asterisk. Cook until vegetables are almost tender. Add okra and corn. Cook 15 minutes longer. Just before serving rub together butter and flour until well blended. Stir into burgoo. Correct seasoning and sprinkle with parsley.

IRISH SODA BREAD

4 c. sifted flour
1/4 c. sugar
3 tsp. baking powder
1 tsp. salt
1/4 c. butter
2 c. raisins

1 1/3 c. buttermilk or sour milk
1 egg
1 tsp. baking soda
1 egg yolk
1 Tbl. water

Heat oven to 375 degrees. Grease deep 2 1/2 quart casserole. Sift dry ingredients together. Add butter and mix to consistency of coarse cornmeal. Stir in raisins. Pour sour milk, egg and soda in small bowl and beat with rotary beater until blended. Add egg mixture to dry ingredients and stir with wooden spoon until well mixed.

Turn out onto well floured board and knead for 3 minutes until smooth. Shape into a ball and place in casserole. With sharp knife make 1/2-inch deep "X" on top of dough. Beat egg yolk and water together and brush top of bread.

Bake 60-65 minutes or until cake tester comes out clean. Let sit in pan 5 minutes before removing to a wire rack to cool.

CITRUS RIND MARMALADE

Freeze all your citrus rind until enough is on hand - about 5 cups.

Cover rind with water and bring to a quick boil; drain and repeat two more times. The last time cook until tender. Grind peel in blender. Make syrup of 2 1/2 cups water and 2 1/2 cups of sugar (to taste). Add the rind and continue boiling, stirring frequently until quite thick and clear. Then add one package of gelatin and bring to a boil. Pour into sterilized jars.

"CLOOTIE PUDDIN" - CLOTH PUDDING

1 1/2 c. flour
2 c. fine dry breadcrumbs
(homemade)
1 c. finely minced suet
1 c. raisins
1/2 c. currants
1/2 c. sugar

1 tsp. cinnamon
1 tsp. mixed spices
1 tsp. baking soda
1 egg
1 1/2 c. buttermilk or ale
cream, lemon sauce or custard
sauce

Mix flour, crumbs, suet, raisins, currants, sugar, cinnamon, spices and soda together in a bowl. Beat egg and add it together with buttermilk to first mixture. Mix to a soft dough. Wet a pudding cloth or quadruple thickness of cheesecloth and wring out well. Dust with flour, place cloth in bowl and spoon mixture into it. Tie cloth securely at top leaving enough room for pudding to expand. Drop onto a rack in a kettle. Add boiling water to come halfway up sides of pudding.

Steam 2 to 2 1/2 hours, replacing boiling water as needed. Serve hot with cream or sauce. Makes 10 to 12 servings.

HOT LEMON AND VANILLA SAUCE

1 c. sugar
2 Tbl. cornstarch
2 c. boiling water
1/4 lb. butter

Strained juice and grated rind
of 2 large lemons
1 tsp. vanilla

Mix together in a saucepan the sugar and cornstarch. Add boiling water gradually, stirring constantly with wooden spoon. Bring to a boil over low heat and continue cooking 5 minutes, stirring constantly. Remove from fire. Add the butter and stir until melted. Add the juice and grated rind of the lemons, and the vanilla. Serve hot on cloth pudding.

FRESH CHURNED BUTTER

Good butter is the result of first rate cream and skillful churning.

It's all in the rhythm. I can't really explain it, but it takes perfect rhythm to churn cream this way.

The equipment used for making butter is often a fine token of folk arts including carved churns, intricately painted cream containers, delicately carved butter molds and stamps.

I churn the butter for my family in an antique countertop churn in the kitchen. One quart of whipping cream yields about one pound of butter and I churn it up in 20-25 minutes. Because it goes rancid fast, I freeze what I can't use right away. It'll keep about two months that way.

At my classes in Greenfield Village, the students take turns churning while seated in front of a large, old wooden churn. If the students have perfect rhythm, they have some delicious fresh butter for their peanut bread. If the rhythm is off, they have thick cream instead.

Butter Prints

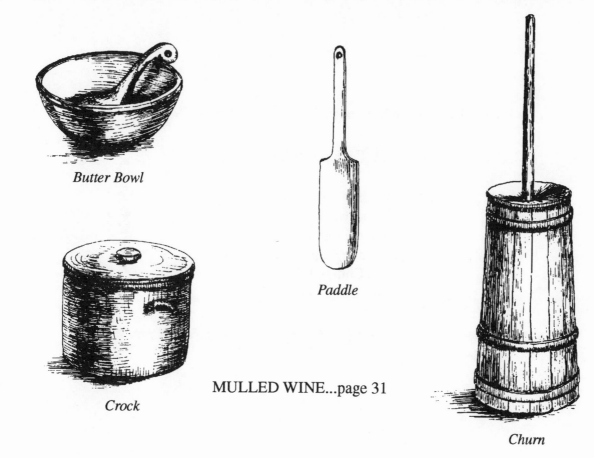

Butter Bowl

Paddle

Crock

MULLED WINE...page 31

Churn

21

FIREPLACE II

Green Onion Bread
Brunswick Stew
Steamed Cider Pudding
Cinnamon Cider Sauce
Fresh Churned Butter
Hot Cider Toddy

GREEN ONION BREAD

4 1/2 c. whole wheat flour
3 c. flour
3 tsp. baking soda
1 tsp. salt
1/3 c. sugar

1/2 lb. plus 2 tsp. butter
2 eggs, slightly beaten
2 1/4 c. buttermilk
Good bunch green onions,
chopped fine

Mix together the first column of ingredients. With fingertips work in butter until mixture resembles coarse meal. Add buttermilk to slightly beaten eggs and beat again. Make well in center of flour mixture and add eggs and buttermilk a little at a time working in with your fingers after each addition to form a stiff dough. Add green onions and knead into dough.

Place dough on lightly floured board and knead about 10 minutes. Divide dough in half. Shape into round loaves and make a crisscross on each loaf with a sharp knife. Brush with slightly beaten egg yolk or milk.

Bake in a dutch oven until done when tested with a straw. Serves 8.

BRUNSWICK STEW

There are many versions of this stew. However, the basic recipe for this version was originated by the women of the Pawhatan, Chickahominy and Cherokee tribes.

1 large chicken	Piece of salt pork
1 rabbit	2 c. fresh corn cut from cob
2 bay leaves, crumbled	2 c. large lima beans
5 peppercorns	6 tomatoes, quartered
3 sprigs parsley	Salt and pepper
1 stalk celery, cut up	1 Tbl. sugar
3 potatoes, cut up	1/2 tsp. oregano
2 large onions, sliced	1/2 tsp. thyme
Pinch of mace	1/2 tsp. savory

Cut salt pork in small pieces and brown slowly in large skillet. Remove salt pork and save. Cut rabbit into serving pieces, dredge in seasoned flour and brown in salt pork fat. Place chicken in large pot, place rabbit on top of chicken. Add salt pork, beans, onions, and celery. Cover with boiling water, cover tightly and simmer 2 hours.

Add other ingredients except tomatoes. Cook until vegetables are just tender. Mix a little flour and water and add to stew. Add tomatoes and cook 5 minutes. Correct seasonings and serve.

STEAMED CIDER PUDDING

2 eggs
1/4 c. sugar
1/4 c. melted butter
1 c. molasses
3 c. flour
1 1/2 tsp. baking soda
1 tsp. cinnamon

3/4 tsp. nutmeg
1/4 tsp. allspice
3/4 tsp. salt
1 c. cider
1 c. currants
1/2 c. chopped dates
1/2 c. raisins

Beat eggs, gradually beat in sugar. Add butter and blend well. Stir in molasses. Combine flour, soda, spices and salt. Add to egg mixture. Add hot cider and mix well. Dust currants, dates and raisins with flour and fold into mixture.

Turn into buttered and floured molds. Cover tightly with wax paper. Place in boiling water, cover and steam. Serve with cinnamon and cider sauce. Serves 12.

CINNAMON CIDER SAUCE

1/2 c. brown sugar
4 Tbl. cornstarch
1/2 tsp. cinnamon
1/2 tsp. freshly grated nutmeg

Dash of salt
2 c. apple cider
2 Tbl. butter

Combine all ingredients but the butter in a saucepan. Cook over low heat stirring constantly until thickened. Stir in butter until well blended. Makes 2 3/4 cups. Serve hot.

HOT CIDER TODDY

2/3 c. honey
7 c. cider
1 apple
Whole cloves

1 orange
1 tsp. grated orange rind
2 c. orange juice

Mix honey and one cup of cider well. Add rest of cider. Stud orange and apple with cloves. Add to cider and heat. Add rind and juice and heat a few minutes longer. Serve piping hot.

FIREPLACE III

Spiced Fish Stew
Peanut Bread
Carrot Pudding
Wine Sauce
Fresh Churned Butter
Mulled Wine

SPICED FISH STEW

1 c. melted butter
6 onions, sliced
3 lbs. fish, cut in cubes
1 lb. oysters
4 c. of fish or chicken broth
4 c. water
*6 tomatoes, quartered
*3/4 c. finely diced salt pork
3 c. noodles

*3 c. diced potatoes
1 lb. shrimp
3/4 c. peeled diced cucumber
3 Tbl. chopped parsley
*1/2 tsp. mace
*1/2 tsp. ground cloves
*1 tsp. fresh, grated nutmeg
*1 tsp. allspice
*Grated rind of lemon

Heat butter in large kettle. Dredge fish in seasoned flour, brown in butter, remove and set aside. Brown onions in butter. Add oysters and cook 5 minutes. Add water and broth and cook 15 minutes. Add *ingredients and reserved fish and simmer 20 minutes or so. Add shrimp, cucumber and parsley, simmer 5 minutes.

Serve from pot with thick slices of homemade bread and lemon wedges. Serves 10-12.

PEANUT BREAD

This is a rich and delicious bread made from the lowly goober.

1/2 c. sugar
3 tsp. baking powder
4 c. flour
1/2 tsp. salt

1 tsp. baking soda
1 1/2 c. milk
1/2 c. corn syrup
1 c. raw peanuts, ground

Preheat oven to 350 degrees. Mix dry ingredients. Mix together milk and corn syrup. Combine dry ingredients with liquids and add peanuts. Form into a round shaped loaf. Place by fire and cook until straw tests clean.

Baking powder was not produced commercially until 1850. Until then, saleratus was used as a lightening agent. Saleratus was obtained from the ashes of burned down corncobs. This had a very strong flavor and was used mostly combined with ginger or molasses.

STEAMED CARROT PUDDING

*1 c. raisins
*1/2 c. currants
*1/2 c. chopped suet
*1 c. packed brown sugar
*1 c. grated carrots (4 raw)
*1 c. grated raw potato

2 tsp. ground ginger
2 tsp. cinnamon
2 tsp. ground cloves
1 whole nutmeg, grated
1 tsp. baking powder
Dash salt
1 1/2 c. flour

Mix all dry ingredients together. In a large bowl mix all other *ingredients. Pour dry ingredients over suet mixture and blend everything well. Pack mixture into well buttered and floured molds. Cover tightly with wax paper. Placed filled mold in pot with boiling water that comes up 3/4 of the way on the side of the mold. Cover pot and steam until done (individual molds about 1 hour, single mold 3-4 hours). Add boiling water to pot as needed. Serve with wine sauce. Serves 10-12.

WINE SAUCE

1 c. brown sugar
1/2 tsp. salt
2 c. hot water

1 c. sweet wine
6 Tbl. cornstarch
4 Tbl. butter

Blend sugar, cornstarch and salt. Slowly add water, stirring constantly. Cook until thickened and clear. Remove from fire and stir in butter. Add wine and blend gently, Serve hot over carrot pudding.

MULLED WINE

*4 thin orange slices
*8 thin lemon slices
*8 cloves
*3 cinnamon sticks
*1/2 freshly grated nutmeg

*1/2 c. sugar
*1/4 c. water
1 bottle red wine
1/2 c. brandy

Place *ingredients in a pot. Bring to a simmer, stirring until sugar is dissolved. Add wine and continue to heat. DO NOT BOIL. Stir in brandy; pour into heated mugs and serve. Serves 8.

Early American Recipes

Chives *Parsley* *Basil*

VICTORIAN

Steak and Kidney Pie
English Puff Pastry
Mashed Potatoes
Green Peas with Mint
Trifle
Boiled Custard
Marzipan Fruits
Wassail Bowl

STEAK AND KIDNEY PIE

This dish was always served as our traditional New Year's dinner. However, my father could never wait and we usually were able to cajole my mother into serving some shortly before midnight on New Year's eve. Boy, did it taste great.

**Round steak or leftover chuck
or roast beef
Beef kidney
Pork or meat link sausages**

**Flour
Salt and pepper to taste
Water**

Cook meat and kidney; cool. Cut meat in 1 to 2-inch pieces. Slice kidney. Combine flour, salt and pepper. Lightly coat meat, kidney and sausage with seasoned flour. Place sausage in bottom of pie dish, cover with meat and kidney. Cover with puff pastry. Pour water through vent in pastry, continuing to add while cooking as needed. Bake at 350 degrees, till pastry is golden brown.

Instead of plain water I will often use commercial powdered gravy mix in order to have a nice thick gravy in the pie when it is ready to serve. However, extra water may have to be added as the flour tends to make the gravy quite thick.

RUFF PUFF PASTRY OR ENGLISH PUFF PASTRY

(For many meat, poultry, and game pies)

2 1/4 c. flour
1/4 tsp. salt
3/4 c. lard or butter

Dash lemon juice
Ice water

Mix the flour and salt and add the lard or butter. Cut into pieces the size of large cherries. Mix and blend well. Make a well in the center and add lemon juice and just enough ice water to make an elastic dough. Press into a ball and chill for 15 minutes.

Place on a floured board and roll into a long strip. Fold away from yourself into three folds. Seal the edges with the rolling pin and turn the pastry around so that the folded edges are to your right and left. Roll again and fold. Chill for 15 minutes. Repeat the process and chill another 15 minutes. Then repeat once more and chill the dough until needed.

To prevent milk from sticking to the pan during scalding, first rinse the pan with very cold water.

MASHED POTATOES

6 to 8 medium-size potatoes,
peeled and quartered
6 Tbl. butter

Salt and freshly ground pepper
1/2 c. hot cream

Boil the potatoes. Drain and dry. Either put through a food mill or ricer, or mash with a masher. They can be prepared in an electric mixer if you have a paddle attachment. Add the butter and mash again. Add the seasonings and hot cream and beat with a wooden spatula or spoon until light and thoroughly blended. Reheat for a moment over hot water and serve in a heated serving dish topped with a lump of softened butter, unless you are serving gravy.

When a recipe calls for bouquet garni or spices to be placed in a cheesecloth, keep several tea balls handy. Place the herbs or spices in a tea ball and place in the pot. The tea ball can be washed, dried and used over and over.

GREEN PEAS WITH MINT

3 lbs. peas in the pod	1 sprig fresh mint
1 tsp. sugar	2 tsp. butter
Boiling salted water	Salt and pepper

Pod peas. Place in a pan of boiling salted water with mint and sugar. Boil gently until tender, 5-7 minutes. Strain. Shake gently in butter and seasoning. If frozen peas must be used, try cooking them as follows:

1 package frozen peas	1/2 Tbl. butter
Salt and pepper	Fresh mint

Put butter and frozen peas in saucepan with tight fitting lid. Heat gently, shaking pan from time to time so that peas will heat through. When they are good and warm, remove lid to allow unwanted moisture to escape. Season and serve with fresh chopped mint sprinkled on top of peas.

TRIFLE

This was always the dessert my mother served for our traditional Christmas Dinner. Even now Christmas never seems complete without this delicious dessert.

The trifle was brought to America by the British Colonists. In this country, the wine-soaked cake was also known as tipsy squire and tipsy parson.

Place a layer of spongecake in a crystal bowl. Saturate it with sherry, rum, or brandy. Stud with 1/2 c. toasted almonds, then refrigerate until serving time. Make custard. Combine 1 c. heavy cream with 1 Tb. confectioners sugar and 1 tsp. vanilla, then beat until stiff. Before serving, pour custard over spongecake, then pile whipped cream on top. Jam may be spread over the cake before the custard and cream are added. I always spread the spongecake with raspberry jam before saturating it with sherry - the jam is easier to spread on dry cake rather than after it has been soaked. Serves 6-8.

BOILED CUSTARD
(Soft custard)

6 egg yolks
1/2 c. sugar
1/4 tsp. salt

3 c. light cream
2 tsp. vanilla

In the top pan of a double boiler combine the egg yolks, sugar and salt. In another saucepan heat the cream just until it steams, and stir it very slowly into the yolk mixture. Cook over (but not touching) simmering water, stirring constantly until the mixture coats a metal spoon. Remove the pan from over the hot water and stir in the vanilla. Cool the custard and chill it. Pour it into 6 individual serving dishes or serve it as a sauce over cake or with pudding. Milk may be substituted for cream in this recipe. A thicker custard may be achieved by reducing the cream or milk content.

When using eggs to thicken, curdling can be prevented by pouring a small amount of hot mixture slowly into the beaten eggs, beating constantly. Then combine with the remaining hot liquid.

MARZIPAN FRUITS

1 c. almond paste (1/2 lb.)	**4 tsp. white corn syrup**
1 c. powdered sugar	**1/2 tsp. vanilla**

Place almond paste into a bowl and knead. Add sugar gradually. Continue kneading, adding syrup and flavor. Do not over mix. Mixture should feel like heavy pie dough. Use cornstarch to dust table and keep marzipan from sticking. Separate into pieces and color for fruit.

Now use your imagination to form oranges, strawberries, bananas, apples and grapes. It even looks great formed into pea pods, carrots, green peppers and just about anything you have the talent to make.

These "fruits" were usually served after dinner along with a glass of sherry. They were, and remain today, a delicacy.

WASSAIL BOWL

*4 c. apple cider
*1/2 tsp. grated nutmeg
*1 tsp. ground ginger
*2-inch cinnamon stick
*3 whole cloves
*6 whole allspice

2 bottles sherry
20 oz. pale ale
2 c. sugar
Whole cloves
2 fresh red apples
1 orange (if desired)

Combine *ingredients, bring to a boil and simmer 10 minutes. Strain. Add sherry, ale and sugar. Stir over low heat until sugar dissolves. Pour into heat proof punch bowl. Stud each orange and apple with 3 or 4 cloves and float in wassail bowl. A small bottle of cranberry juice may be added to the punch bowl if desired. Makes 25-30 servings.

This is a traditional English beverage and at the Christmas Season there is always at least one Wassail Feast. At the holiday season I often have friends in to help recreate an English Wassail Party.

Originally the wassail bowl was carried into the great feasting hall high on the shoulders of the men servants all the guests raising their glasses in salute calling "Hail Wassail", "Hail Wassail."

PLANTATION

Chicken Mold with Almonds
Carrot Mold
Green Beans and Sauteed Mushrooms
Spoon Bread
Chess Pies with Fresh Whipped Cream
Pie Crust Pastry
Sangaree

CHICKEN MOLD WITH ALMONDS

This dish has a richness of flavor that was favored by many of the housewives of French descent in the mid-nineteenth century. This particular version is from South Carolina.

5-6 lb. chicken	1/2 c. plus 1 Tbl. butter
*1 onion, cut up	1/2 c. plus 1 Tbl. flour
*1 bay leaf	1 1/2 c. heavy cream
*1 bouquet garni of thyme and	Salt and cayenne to taste
parsley	2 egg yolks
*1 Tbl. salt	2 tsp. lemon juice
*8 peppercorns	2 Tbl. blanched almonds
1 c. blanched almonds	lightly sauteed in butter

Cook chicken in a large pot with a tight fitting lid. Place chicken in pot with enough water to just cover chicken. Then add the *ingredients. Cook until chicken is tender. Remove chicken and strain broth saving 1 1/2 cups.

Take meat from chicken discarding skin and bones. Grind meat fine with 1 cup of blanched almonds. Beat the egg yolks and lemon juice into mixture and set aside. Heat butter in heavy skillet then add flour and blend. Add the 1 1/2 cups of chicken stock and cook, stirring constantly, until smooth and thick. Add cream and cook 5 minutes more. Season to taste with salt and cayenne. Add 1 cup of this sauce to chicken mixture. Blend and correct seasoning. Turn into a buttered 2 qt. ring mold and set in a pan with 1 inch of hot water.

Bake 1 hour at 325 degrees or until set. Cover top with foil if it browns too fast. Allow to set in mold for 5 minutes after removing from oven. Sprinkle with sauteed almonds.

CARROT MOLD

Carrots were used mainly in soups and stews in the eighteenth century. However, this mold was made in Charleston and was served with veal or chicken.

2 c. mashed, cooked, carrots
2 well beaten eggs
1/2 c. heavy cream
1/2 tsp. salt

1/4 tsp. pepper
1 good pinch nutmeg
2 tsp. sugar

Scrape carrots, slice and cook until tender in slightly sweetened water. Drain, mash and measure two cups. Combine carrots and eggs, then beat in cream and seasonings.

Turn into 1 quart buttered ring mold. Set mold in pan of water and bake at 375 degrees 30 minutes or until set. Unmold onto warm serving plate. If desired fill center with minted green leaves. Serves 6.

GREEN BEANS WITH MUSHROOMS

2 c. sliced fresh mushrooms
4 Tbl. butter
6 c. cooked green beans

1/2 tsp. summer savory
1/2 tsp. salt
1/4 tsp. pepper

Wash string beans and snap into 1-inch pieces. Place the beans in a pot and add summer savory and salt. Cover with water and cook until tender.

While beans are cooking:

Wash and towel dry mushrooms and then slice. Melt butter in heavy skillet. Add mushrooms, season with a little salt and pepper. Saute mushrooms until golden brown.

Drain green beans well. Gently toss green beans and mushrooms together. Green beans and mushrooms may be served in the center of a carrot ring. Serves 12.

SPOON BREAD

Southern spoon bread should have more of a pudding texture rather than a bread.

1 c. cornmeal
1 1/2 tsp. salt
2 Tbl. butter
2 c. boiling water
4 egg yolks, beaten

1/2 c. milk
1/2 c. flour
4 tsp. baking powder
4 egg whites, beaten stiff
1 Tbl. sugar

Stir together cornmeal, salt, butter and boiling water. Add egg yolks beaten with milk. Mix flour, sugar and baking powder together. Add this to cornmeal mixture and stir. Beat egg whites until stiff and fold gently into bread batter. Pour mixture into a buttered 2 quart baking dish -- one that is deep enough so that mixture only half fills the dish.

Bake 30-45 minutes in a 375 degree oven. Serve with fresh butter.

CHESS PIE

Makes pastry for two 9-inch pies

1/2 c. butter
1 c. sugar
3 egg yolks, beaten thick
1 egg white, beaten stiff
Whipping cream

1 c. chopped nuts*
1 c. seedless raisins*
1 tsp. vanilla*
1/2 tsp. salt*

Make 12 patty shells from pastry dough. Cream butter and sugar, beat in egg yolks. Fold in egg whites and stir until mixture is foamy. Add *ingredients and stir until well mixed.

Fill patty shells and bake at 400 degrees until mixture sets. Reduce heat to 350 degrees and bake until golden brown (15-20 minutes in all). Serve topped with slightly sweetened whipped cream.

PIE CRUST PASTRY

This pastry recipe has been used in my family for many generations. I first watched my grandmother make the most mouth watering fruit pies using this pastry and later learned how to make it from my mother.

Nine-inch double crust

2 c. flour	**1/4 c. cold water**
1 tsp. salt	**2/3 c. lard**

Blend salt and flour together. Place approximately 1/3 c. of this mixture in small bowl. Add 1/4 cup cold water, stir to form a paste, set aside. Cut 2/3 cups lard into dry flour mixture and work with fingertips until mixture resembles course cornmeal.

Stir flour paste into lard and flour mixture. Work with your hand until ingredients are well incorporated and dough forms a ball. Divide dough in half and roll out on well floured pastry cloth. Always turn the dough never the rolling pin, and do not be afraid to handle pastry.

SANGAREE

The essential characteristic of sangaree is its deep red-color, derived from red wine. (Sang is from the French word meaning blood). In Colonial days, this mild drink was valued as a bracer.

2 qt. strawberries, crushed　　　　**1/2 c. lemon juice**
1 c. sugar　　　　　　　　　　　　**1/2 gal. red wine**
Sparkling water

Combine all ingredients, except sparkling water, mix well and chill for 1 hour. Strain. Half fill glasses with wine mixture and add sparkling water to taste.

CREOLE

Calalou
Skillet Eggplant and Corn
Baked Turnip and Potato Puff
Louisiana Honey Bread
Creole Fritters with Fresh Whipped Cream
Southern Spiced Tea

CALALOU

In early days, pork was almost always available either fresh or cured. This recipe is one concocted by the housewives of Martinique.

3 lbs. cooked pork cut in 1-inch pieces
3 cloves garlic, chopped
3 green peppers, chopped
1 large eggplant, peeled and cubed
1 lb. okra, sliced
3 c. corn cut from cob
6 green onions, chopped
1 small red pepper pod

4 c. pumpkin, peeled, seeded and cubed
3 qts. chicken broth
*2 c. chopped celery
*4 c. cucumber peeled, seeded, diced
*Salt and pepper to taste
*Dash hot pepper sauce
*2 c. fresh minced parsley
*1 tsp. file powder
*8 c. cooked rice

Combine in large heavy pot all ingredients except those with a *. Bring to a boil, cover and simmer until vegetables are almost tender. Add celery, cook 15 minutes. Add cucumber, cook 15 minutes. Add salt, pepper, hot pepper sauce and parsley. Remove from heat, stir in file powder.

Serve from deep bowl accompanied by rice. Serves 8-10.

File powder was an important ingredient introduced by the Choctow Indians. It was made from the dried pulverized leaves of the sassafrass plant. The Choctaws used it medicinally, but the Negro cooks used it as a thickening agent for their superb gumbos, thick soups and stews.

SKILLET EGGPLANT AND CORN

1 medium size eggplant	Salt
3 ears of fresh corn	Pepper
3 Tbl. oil	3 Tbl. minced fresh herbs
12-15 cherry tomatoes	(parsley, chives, basil)
3 Tbl. butter	

Do not peel eggplant. Cut into 3/4-inch slices then cube. Cut corn from cob. In a good size skillet with tight fitting lid heat oil to almost smoking. Toss in eggplant and brown on all sides. Lessen heat and add corn kernels. Cut tomatoes into halves and add. Break butter into small pieces and scatter over top of vegetables. Sprinkle with salt and pepper. Cover tightly and cook gently for about 20 minutes, shaking the pan from time to time. Test eggplant; it should be firm and the corn should be tender.

Serve sprinkled with herbs. Makes 6-8 servings.

The intermarriage of the Spanish and French produced a people known as Creoles. The mixing of the two cultures created Creole cookery. However, the Choctaw Indians and the Negro slave did much to influence this unique cuisine as they provided such ingredients as rice, sugar, shrimp, crab, pecans and red fish.

BAKED POTATO AND TURNIP PUFF

2 c. hot mashed potatoes
2 c. hot mashed turnip
2 Tbl. melted butter
1/2 tsp. salt

1/8 tsp. pepper
2 Tbl. sweet cream
1 egg, well beaten

Mix potato and turnip. Add other ingredients in order given. Turn into a well-greased baking dish and bake in a hot oven at 400 degrees for 20 minutes.

Serve hot from dish that puff has been cooked in. Serves 6.

From 1727-1751 France sent shiploads of "casket girls" to become the brides of men in the new Louisiana colony. They were so called because the French government gave them small caskets containing household and clothing articles.

LOUISIANA HONEY BREAD

This is a very old and unusual bread and is most delicious.

2 c. flour
1 tsp. baking soda
1 tsp. baking powder
1 tsp. salt
1 tsp. ginger

1/2 tsp. cinnamon
1 c. milk
1 c. honey
1 egg, slightly beaten

Mix together all dry ingredients. Add milk, honey and egg. Mix this for at least 30 minutes. Spoon into greased and floured loaf pan. Heat oven to 375 degrees, Bake 45 minutes.
Serve thinly sliced and well buttered.

In 1755, many Cajun French Canadians settled in Louisiana. The word cajun was derived from slurring the sounds in the word Acadian, since these people were from Acadia -- now Nova Scotia.

CREOLE FRITTERS

Fritters are light batter-covered shellfish or fruit fried cakes. They were often flavored with rum or brandy. When they are made well they are a delight. This batter is for fruit.

2 eggs, separated
1 c. flour
1 Tbl. melted butter
1/4 tsp. salt
2 Tbl. brandy
6 Tbl. water
Lard or oil for frying

3 bananas, peeled, cut
lengthwise twice and crosswise
in thirds
Peeled and sliced apples or
peaches
Orange sections
Large strawberries
Pineapple slices

Beat egg yolks until lemon colored. Beat in flour. Add butter, salt, brandy and water. The batter should be thick enough to coat but not heavy, about the consistency of thick cream. Beat egg whites until stiff and fold into batter.

Heat fat or oil to about 375 degrees. Dip fruit in batter (be sure it is all covered). Fry to golden brown, drain on paper towel. Continue until all are done. Place on serving plate and sift confectioners sugar over all and serve hot.

Serve as a light dessert with fresh whipped cream if desired. Makes 12 servings.

SOUTHERN SPICED TEA

This is a very popular refreshment around Charleston, S. Carolina. It can be served hot in winter or iced in summer.

4 c. boiling water	**Juice of 3 oranges**
3 Tbl. tea leaves	**1 tsp. whole cloves**
Juice of 1/2 lemon	**4 c. cold water**
1 c. sugar	

Pour boiling water over the tea leaves. Let stand for a few minutes, then strain. Boil together sugar, whole cloves and water until it becomes a thin syrup. Strain this into tea, add orange and lemon juice.

Serve with lemon slices. Makes about 2 quarts.

As well as being delicious food, gumbo was the name applied to the dialect spoken by the Negroes of Louisiana. It is also another name for okra.

NORTHWESTERN

Beef Fruit Stew
Egg Dumplings
Baked Stuffed Potatoes
Prune Bread
Miracle Meringue Cake
Red Wine Punch

OREGON BEEF FRUIT STEW

This is a most unusual stew that makes use of the abundance of dried fruits found in the Northwestern states.

3 Tbl. fat	1/2 c. prunes
2 1/2 lbs. beef cut in cubes	1 tsp. sugar
3 c. cider	1 slice lemon with rind
4 onions	1/8 tsp. pepper
1/2 c. dried apricots	3 Tbl. flour
	3 Tbl. butter

Melt fat and brown beef on all sides. Add cider, lower heat. Peel onions and add to stew. Wash apricots and prunes, sprinkle them over stew then add sugar, lemon slice and pepper.

Simmer 2 hrs. or until meat is tender. Mix flour and butter together, stir into stew. Cook several minutes until thickened.

Serve with baked Idaho potatoes or dumplings. Serves 4-6.

EGG DUMPLINGS

2 c. flour
1 tsp. salt
4 tsp. baking powder
1/4 tsp. pepper

1 egg, well beaten
3 Tbl. butter, melted
Milk to make a stiff batter

Blend dry ingredients; then add melted butter, egg and just enough milk to make a moist stiff batter. Plop by tablespoonfuls into boiling liquid. Cook gently, covered, for 15 minutes.

BAKED STUFFED POTATOES

4 baking potatoes
*6 Tbl. butter
*1 tsp. salt
*1/4 tsp. pepper

4 green onions, chopped
1/2 c. fine bread crumbs
*Grated fresh nutmeg
2 Tbl. butter

Bake potatoes at 400 degrees about 45 minutes or until fork tender. Cut a slice lengthwise from top of each. Scoop out and mash potatoes with *ingredients. Fold in green onions. Replace in shells. Sprinkle with breadcrumbs and dot with butter. Bake at 375 degrees until golden brown.

PRUNE BREAD

1 c. flour
1/2 c. whole wheat flour
1/2 tsp. baking soda
1/2 tsp. baking powder
1/2 tsp. salt
1/2 c. sugar

1 egg, lightly beaten
2 Tbl. butter, melted
1/2 c. milk
1/2 c. chopped cooked prunes
1/2 c. prune juice

Preheat oven to 375 degrees. Mix together dry ingredients. Mix together egg, butter, milk, prunes and juice. Add dry ingredients and blend well. Spoon into buttered 9x5 loaf pan. Bake for about 40 minutes or until done when tested.

When baking yeast breads, have all ingredients at room temperature since variations in the temperature will kill the yeast action.

MIRACLE MERINGUE CAKE

This is one of the most unusual cakes I have ever made and it can be kept well in the refrigerator for a week. I think it improves with age.

CAKE

1/2 c. butter
1/2 c. sugar
4 egg yolks
1/4 c. half & half

1/2 tsp. vanilla
1 c. sifted cake flour
1 1/4 tsp. baking powder
1/8 tsp. salt

Cream butter with sugar until it is very light. Add egg yolks one at a time beating after each addition. Mix in half & half. Add vanilla. Sift the salt, flour and baking powder onto a piece of wax paper. Add it to the cream mixture a little at a time, beating well after each addition and beating for at least two minutes. Grease and flour two 9-inch cake pans. Spread batter in pans.

MERINGUE

4 egg whites
Pinch of salt
1 c. sugar

1 tsp. vanilla
1/4 c. broken walnuts or pecans

Beat egg whites until stiff, add salt. Gradually add sugar and continue beating, add vanilla. Spread on top of both pans of batter. Sprinkle one cake with the nuts. Bake at 325 degrees for about 35 minutes or until light brown. Watch carefully so cake doesn't burn. Set pans on a wire rack. Allow cakes to cool in their pans. (continued on next page)

FILLING

1/2 lb. dried apricots	**Sugar**
2 c. water	**1 c. heavy cream**

    While cakes are cooling make filling. Cook the apricots in the water. Simmer for about 25 minutes or until fruit is tender. Add sugar to taste, usually about 1 c. Boil 5 more minutes. Mash fruit or put through a food mill. Cool fruit thoroughly. Whip cream and fold into fruit.

    Remove cakes from pans. Place the one without the nuts, meringue side down on a plate. Spread cake part with 2/3 of the filling. Place the other cake on top with the meringue side up. Place small circle of reserved filling on top of meringue.

I will often use fresh strawberries crushed and folded into the whipped cream for my filling. Then I place fresh whole strawberries on top of the meringue. This looks beautiful as well as tastes delicious.

RED WINE PUNCH

*1 1/2 pts. red wine
*1 pt. of freshly made tea
Juice of 2 lemons, strained

*1/2 c. rum
*3/4 c. sugar
Finely shredded peel of half a lemon

Mix together *ingredients and bring almost to a boil. Add lemon peel and lemon juice just before serving. This punch may be served hot or cold.

IRISH

Boiled Irish Ham
Creamed Cabbage
Colcannon
Irish Drop Scones
Irish Coffee Pudding
Irish Lemonade

BOILED IRISH HAM

1 ham
1 qt. Irish stout
1/2 c. sugar
*1 wisp of fresh hay
(impossible in the city, I know)

Enough cold water to cover the
ham
2 Tbl. breadcrumbs
2 Tbl. brown sugar
Cloves

Soak the ham in cold water for 24 hours to soften. Put it into a large pot with the stout, sugar, and hay and add enough water to cover the ham. Bring very slowly to a boil and simmer, at the bubble, allowing 20 to 25 minutes to the pound. If the ham is cooked too fast, it will become tough and stringy.

At the end of the cooking time turn off the heat and let the ham set for at least a half-hour in the liquid. Now take it out of the pot and wipe off the skin. Cover the fat with the bread crumbs and sugar mixed together. Stud generously with cloves and return to a hot oven to color (for cold ham, you should let the joint cool completely in the liquid and do not color in the oven.)

*The addition of the hay (is your husband a farmer?) makes a sweet country smell in the kitchen.

CREAMED CABBAGE

1 white cabbage,
approximately 2 lbs.
Boiling water
1 1/2 Tbl. butter
1 Tbl. flour

Salt and pepper
1/2 grated nutmeg
1 c. evaporated milk

Quarter the cabbage and cut away the tough stalk. Plunge the quartered cabbage into a pan of fast-boiling salted water. Cook for 5 minutes (with the lid off). Drain well and refresh under the cold faucet. Cut the quarters, across the grain, in 1/2-inch strips.

Melt the butter in a saucepan and add the shredded cabbage. Stir it around the melted butter. Sprinkle in the flour, salt and pepper, and the nutmeg, and stir well with a wooden spoon, so that the flour is mixed. Add the evaporated milk and bring to a boil. Put the lid on the saucepan and cook very gently for 30 minutes. You may stir from time to time, in case it might burn. This is very good. Makes 6 servings.

Food that has been over salted can often be disguised by adding a little sugar or a small amount of vinegar.

COLCANNON

Traditionally, colcannon is always served at Hallow's Eve. A miniature thimble and horseshoe, a button, a silver sixpence (dime), and a wedding ring are each wrapped in white paper and dropped into the mixture. These forecast the fortunes of the finders. If your portion contains the ring, you will marry and live happily ever after. The silver sixpence denotes wealth, the horseshoe good fortune, thimble a spinster, and the button a bachelor.

6-8 potatoes	**1 Tbl. butter**
1 1/2 c. milk	**1 Tbl. chopped parsley**
6 scallions (green onions)	**Pepper and salt**
1 1/2 c. boiled green cabbage	
or curly kale	

Boil the potatoes and mash. Add the boiling milk and chopped scallions and beat until fluffy. Toss the cooked cabbage, finely chopped, gently in the melted butter. Add to the potatoes, together with the parsley, and fold well. Season generously with pepper and taste for salt.

This is very Irish and far nicer than it sounds. In some districts the cabbage is omitted. 6-8 servings.

IRISH DROP SCONES

1 c. flour	2 Tbl. butter
1/2 tsp. baking soda	1 egg
1 tsp. baking powder	1 Tbl. Irish golden syrup or
1/4 tsp. cream of tartar	corn syrup
2 Tbl. sugar	5 Tbl. milk

Mix together dry ingredients. Cut butter into dry ingredients. Work with fingertips until mixture resembles coarse cornmeal. Beat egg lightly, add milk and syrup. Stir liquid ingredients into flour mixture. Batter should be able to be dropped from spoon.

Allow batter to rest for 15 minutes. Drop from teaspoon onto oiled griddle. Cook about 3 minutes on each side. Wrap scones in clean cloth to keep them soft. Makes about 20.

A piece of brown paper or paper towel laid briefly on top of hot soup after skimming will absorb all remaining grease.

IRISH COFFEE PUDDING

6 eggs
3/4 c. sugar
1 c. very strong black coffee
2 1/2 Tbl. unflavored gelatin

1/3 c. Irish whiskey
1 1/4 c. heavy cream
2 Tbl. crushed walnuts

Separate yolks from whites of eggs. Cream yolks with sugar. Heat coffee and dissolve gelatin in hot coffee. Add this to egg yolk and sugar mixture beating constantly. Put this mixture in top of double boiler and place over boiling water. Continue beating this mixture until it begins to thicken. Add whiskey and beat until mixture is thick and creamy.

Remove from heat and place over ice beating constantly until mixture is at point of setting. Whip cream and fold it into mixture. Fold in well beaten egg whites. Put a 3-inch collar of wax paper on a 7-inch souffle dish. Pour mixture into souffle dish. Oil jar and push down into center of pudding. Allow to set.

Remove paper collar by easing around the circumference with a knife dipped in hot water. Do same to remove jar.

Fill center with:

1 c. cream whipped and sweetened mixed with 2 Tbl. chopped walnuts
Decorate exposed sides of pudding with crushed walnuts that you press on with the palm of your hand.

IRISH LEMONADE

3 lemons
2 c. sugar

1 Tbl. tartaric or citric acid
3 c. boiling water

Squeeze juice from lemons. Put juice, lemon skins, sugar, acid and boiling water into jug. Stir well to dissolve sugar. Cover jug and allow to cool. Discard lemon skins and bottle liquid. To serve put 2 Tbl. liquid into glass. Fill with ice and soda water.

PENNSYLVANIA DUTCH I

Boova Shenkel
Schnitzel Beans
Pickled Eggs and Red Beets
Hot Mustard Bread
Shaker Lemon Pie
Switchel or Haying Water

"BOOVA SHENKEL"
(Boy's legs)

This is one more example of the colorful way the Pennsylvania Dutch named their excellent foods. When this dish is cooked it resembles little boy's chubby legs, so came the name. Don't let this deter you from trying it. It is simply delicious.

3 lbs. beef for stewing
2 tsp. salt
12 medium-size potatoes, washed, pared, and thinly sliced
3 Tbl. butter
1/3 c. minced onion
2 Tbl. minced parsley
1 tsp. salt

1/4 tsp. pepper
3 eggs, beaten
2 1/2 c. sifted flour
2 tsp. baking powder
1/2 tsp. salt
2 Tbl. lard
2 Tbl. shortening
8 to 10 Tbl. cold water

Cut meat into pieces and place in dutch oven. Cover with water, add salt and simmer for 2 hours. Cook potatoes until tender; drain. Mix in butter, onion, parsley, salt and pepper. Add eggs and beat mixture lightly. Set aside. Sift together the flour, baking powder, and 1/2 tsp. salt. Cut in the lard and 2 Tbl. shortening with a pastry blender to two knives. Add water, using only enough to hold dough together. Work quickly; do not over-handle. Shape into a ball. Using 1/2 of the dough, roll on a floured surface into a 10-inch round about 1/8-inch thick.

With a knife or spatula, loosen dough from surface whenever sticking occurs; lift dough and sprinkle flour underneath. Spread 1/2 of the potato filling on 1/2 of each round. Fold dough in half over filling. Press edges together with tines of fork to seal. Set aside. Repeat process for remaining half of dough. Carefully drop the two filled pastries into the boiling broth with meat. Cover and simmer about 25 minutes. Arrange the "Boova Shenkel" on a platter and pour hot "sauce" over pastries. Serve immediately. Makes 8 to 10 servings.

SAUCE

Heat 3 Tbl. butter or drippings. Add 1 c. diced, dry bread; brown on all sides. Stir in 1/2 c. milk.

CUT (SCHNITZEL) BEANS

1 1/2 lbs. green beans, cut in 1-inch pieces	**1 tsp. salt**
	Few grains cayenne pepper
3 slices bacon	**1 c. hot water**
1 Tbl. shortening	**4 medium-size tomatoes, cut in pieces**
3 large onions, sliced	

Dice and fry bacon until crisp. Mix in remaining ingredients except tomatoes and cook, covered over low heat 1 hour. Add the tomatoes and continue cooking 2 hours longer, adding more water if necessary.

PICKLED EGGS AND RED BEETS

2 c. (about 1 lb.) young beets
1/4 c. brown sugar
1/2 c. vinegar
1/2 c. cold water

1/2 tsp. salt
Small piece stick cinnamon
3 or 4 whole cloves
6 hard cooked eggs

Wash beets; cut off leaves and stems, leaving on about 1-inch of the root end. Cook until tender. Drain and skin. Boil together for 10 minutes all remaining ingredients except the eggs. Let beets stand in this liquid for several days. Add whole, hard-cooked, shelled eggs to the liquid and let stand in refrigerator for 2 days.

HOT MUSTARD BREAD

This bread is baked in a 9x9-inch cake pan and cut in thick narrow wedges. It is delicious served hot with lots of fresh butter.

1/2 c. butter
1/2 c. sugar
1 beaten egg
2 1/2 c. flour
2 tsp. baking soda
1 tsp. dry mustard

1 tsp. ground cinnamon
1/2 tsp. ground cloves
1 tsp. salt
1 c. molasses
1 c. hot water

Cream sugar and butter until smooth. Add egg and blend well. Mix together flour, spices, mustard, soda and salt. Combine hot water and molasses. Add molasses mixture and flour mixture alternately to egg mixture, stirring well after each addition. Pour into greased and floured cake pan. Bake at 350 degrees for 35 minutes. Serve hot. Makes 1 loaf.

SHAKER LEMON PIE

This was an old handwritten recipe I found inside some old books my husband purchased at an auction. I have tried for years to find out why a yellow bowl was stipulated but have never really received a satisfactory answer. If anyone really knows please let me know.

3 lemons   4 eggs
1 1/3 c. sugar   1 tsp. arrowroot
Pastry for 2 crusts

This is a very old lemon pie recipe which the early Ohio Shakers fashioned frequently. "Slice two lemons as thin as paper, rind and all. Place them in a bowl (it states, "yellow bowl") and pour over them 2 c. of sugar. Mix well and let stand for 2 hours or better. Then go about making your best pastry for 2 crusts. Line a pie dish with same. Beat 4 eggs together with arrowroot and pour over lemons. Fill unbaked pie shell with this and add top crust with small vents cut to let out stem. Place in hot oven at 450 degrees for 15 minutes and then cut down heat and bake until a silver knife inserted into custard comes out clean."

SWITCHEL OR HAYING WATER

There are several variations of this beverage. However, the original form was made almost like this using ingredients that were always readily available. This drink was always welcomed by the men working in the fields, especially when made with cold water pumped fresh from the well. This refreshing thirst quencher served to cool a man's dusty throat and the natural sugars restored his energy.

1 c. brown sugar	**1/2 c. molasses**
1 c. vinegar	**1 Tbl. ground ginger**
1 qt. cold water	

Combine all ingredients and stir well. Tastes good chilled but may be served without chilling.

Pretzels, which are found everywhere in Pennsylvania Dutch country, are said to represent arms crossed in prayer. Pretzels have a history dating back to the crusades.

PENNSYLVANIA DUTCH II

Dutch Pork Pie
Potato Filling
Red Cabbage and Apples
Molasses Graham Bread
Amish Cake Pie with Fresh Whipped Cream
Mulled Cider

DUTCH PORK PIE

This pie is a lot of work but I think it is well worth the effort!

MEAT

2 lbs. thick sliced loin of pork, diced
1 Tbl. parsley, minced

1 large onion, chopped
1 Tbl. ketchup

Preheat oven to 325 degrees.

Put 1/3 of the pork into a deep 2 qt. baking dish and cover with parsley. Add another 1/3 of the pork, spread onion over this layer. Add remaining pork and spread with ketchup.

SAUCE

2 Tbl. butter
2 Tbl. flour
1 3/4 c. milk

1/2 tsp. salt
1/8 tsp. pepper
3 Tbl. bread crumbs

Melt butter over low heat, stir in flour, and add milk slowly, stirring until sauce thickens. Add salt and pepper. Spoon this over pork. Sprinkle breadcrumbs over the top. Bake 1 1/2 hours.

PASTRY

2 c. flour
1/2 tsp. salt

1/3 c. pork fat or lard
1/4 c. water

Mix flour, salt and pork fat until mealy. Add enough water to moisten enough until pastry leaves sides of bowl. Roll out to 1/2-inch thick to cover pie. Return pie to oven and bake 25-30 minutes until crust is brown. Serves 6.

For an infant's cold, roast an onion wrapped in a wet cloth on hot ashes until soft. Peeling the outside off and mashing them, apply on a cloth to the hollow of the baby's feet.

POTATO FILLING

This is one of the most interesting potato dishes I have found in some time. Don't let the combination of ingredients discourage you, it's good!

4 large potatoes	1/2 tsp. salt
1 onion	Pepper to taste
2 Tbl. butter	1/2 c. hot milk mixed with:
3 slices bread, cubed	1/2 c. chicken broth
3 Tbl. minced parsley	1 beaten egg
3 Tbl. chopped celery leaves	2 Tbl. butter

Cut peeled potatoes in eighths and cook in boiling salted water until soft. Meanwhile, saute onion in butter and as it begins to brown add the bread cubes and brown them also.

When potatoes are done, drain and mash. Add bread mixture, parsley leaves, celery, salt and pepper. Add liquid gradually and beat all together. Add beaten egg and beat until mixture is well blended. Put mixture into a greased baking dish and dot with butter. Bake 30 minutes at 350 degrees. Serve with chicken pot pie -- serves 6.

RED CABBAGE WITH APPLES

This recipe was given to me by a farm family I met while camping in Pennsylvania. It is typical of York, Pennsylvania and had been used by this family for generations.

2 1/2 lbs. red cabbage
2 slices salt pork
1 tsp salt
1/8 tsp. pepper
1/2 c. vinegar

1/4 tsp. ground cloves
1/2 tsp. ground allspice
1/2 c. sugar
3 large apples

Dice salt pork and brown in dutch oven. Remove salt pork and set aside. Slice cabbage and place in pot with pork fat. Add all other ingredients except apples and vinegar. Barely cover with water, cover and bring to a boil. Lower heat and cook until almost tender. Add vinegar and continue cooking 10-15 minutes.

Add apples which have been peeled, sliced and cored. Cook about 5 minutes longer until apples are just soft but not mushy. Drain and serve with hot pork. Serves 6-8.

MOLASSES GRAHAM BREAD

1/4 c. sugar
2 c. flour
2 tsp. baking soda
2 tsp. salt
1 tsp. baking powder

1 3/4 c. graham flour
1/3 c. butter
2 eggs, beaten
1 3/4 c. sour or buttermilk
3/4 c. molasses

Mix together dry ingredients, then cut in the butter. Work with fingertips until mixture resembles coarse cornmeal. Blend eggs, milk and molasses. Pour into dry mixture and stir just enough to blend. Pour into two greased and floured loaf pans. Bake at 350 degrees for about 40 minutes.

This bread is most flavorful served hot with fresh butter. It keeps well and can be frozen.

AMISH CAKE PIE

This cake pie dates bake to the 1820s and is most interesting.

Prepare pie dough and line 2 pie pans.

JUICE

1/2 tsp. baking soda	1/2 c. molasses
1 c. hot water	1/2 tsp. vanilla
1/2 c. sugar	1 egg

Mix soda in hot water and set aside. Combine all other juice ingredients and add soda and water mixture. Stir and pour into pie shells.

CAKE

1 c. sugar	1/2 c. milk
1/4 c. butter and lard mixed	1 1/2 c. flour
1 egg	1/2 tsp. baking soda

Beat sugar, butter and lard until fluffy. Add egg and milk and beat well. Blend in flour and soda. Drop batter by spoonfuls into juice in pie pans. Place pies in cold oven and set at 375 degrees. Test after cooking 1/2 hour. Pie top should be brown. Serve with fresh slightly sweetened whipped cream.

MULLED CIDER

1/2 gal. cider
6 whole allspice berries
6 whole cloves

2 sticks cinnamon
1 c. firmly packed brown sugar

Measure cider and brown sugar in saucepan and mix well. Add cinnamon sticks. Place cloves and allspice berries in cheesecloth and add to mixture. Bring to a boil and cook for 5 minutes. Remove spices and serve in heated mugs.

Pennsylvania Dutch cooking has changed little since 1700.

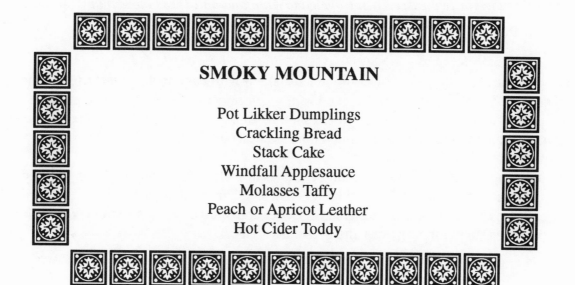

SMOKY MOUNTAIN

Pot Likker Dumplings
Crackling Bread
Stack Cake
Windfall Applesauce
Molasses Taffy
Peach or Apricot Leather
Hot Cider Toddy

POT LIKKER DUMPLINGS

This originated in Tennessee, then traveled to Alabama and Texas more than 100 years ago.

You must have one large pot of turnip greens boiled with ham hocks. Start from scratch, with turnip greens fresh out of the patch and smoked hambone or hocks. Or use chopped turnip greens canned, simmering an hour with the ham, which should already be boiled tender. Mix 2 Tbl. minced onion (fresh, young ones with part of the green tops are best) into 1 1/2 c. unsifted cornmeal. Season with 1/2 tsp. salt and 1/4 tsp. black pepper.

Stir in enough boiling pot liquor from the greens to make a stiff dough. When slightly cooled, mix in one egg thoroughly. Take this by spoonfuls and shape into small patties about 1/2-inch thick. Lay them gently on top of the simmering greens. Cover and simmer 10 or 15 minutes until done. I will often use a combination of turnip greens and mustard greens.

CRACKLING BREAD

The skins and residue left from the rendering of pork fat at hog-killing time make cracklings. Ask a Southerner whose memory goes back far enough about crackling bread crumbled up in buttermilk--and watch his eyes light up!

2 c. cornmeal
1 tsp. baking powder

1/2 tsp. salt
2/3 c. cracklings

Sift into a bowl, cornmeal, baking powder, and salt. Pour into this enough boiling water to make a stiff batter. Add cracklings. (Meat skins packaged for canapes make a passable substitute; one whole cup plus bacon drippings.) Mold into oval shapes (pones), and bake in hot (425 degree) oven, until light brown. Serve with tall glasses of very cold buttermilk, and instructions that the hot crackling bread is to be broken into the milk and eaten with iced teaspoons.

STACK CAKE

This cake is really good and appears to improve the next day, if you are lucky enough to have any left. I sometimes serve fresh whipped cream along with this cake.

3/4 c. shortening
1 c. sugar
1 c. sorghum molasses
3 eggs
1 c. milk

4 c. wheat flour
2 tsp. baking powder
1/2 tsp. soda
1 tsp. salt

Sift well the flour, salt, soda, and baking powder. Cream shortening. Then add sugar a little at a time, blending well. Add sorghum and mix thoroughly. Add eggs one at a time, beating well until smooth. Pour 1/3-inch deep in greased 9-inch pans and bake. This will make 6 or 7 layers. When cool, stack layers using around 3 c. sweetened, slightly spiced applesauce. Commercial applesauce may be used. However I prefer the windfall applesauce following this recipe.

WINDFALL APPLE SAUCE

Cut apples, peels and all. Place in pot and add small piece of cinnamon and a small amount of water. Cook covered for 20 minutes. Cool slightly and add:

1 Tbl. butter per qt.　　　　　　　　　**Grated lemon peel**
Grated nutmeg　　　　　　　　　　　　　**Ground cloves**
Ginger

Add all the above ingredients except the butter to taste. Cool and serve.

MOLASSES TAFFY

This candy is not only good to eat but in the old days the making of it contributed to entertainment. The harder the taffy is pulled the lighter it gets, and taffy pulls were as popular years ago among the young sets as disco sessions are today.

4 c. molasses	4 Tbl. butter or margarine
1 c. brown sugar	1/2 tsp. baking soda
1/2 c. water	1/8 tsp. salt

Combine molasses, sugar, and water in heavy saucepan. Cook over low heat, stirring frequently until candy thermometer reads 272 degrees or until a small amount of the mixture cracks when dropped in cold water. Remove from heat, add butter, soda, and salt. Stir just enough to blend. Pour into a large shallow, buttered pan and allow to stand until cool enough to handle. Butter the fingers and gather taffy into a ball. Pull the candy, using fingertips, until it is firm and light yellow in color. Stretch out into a long rope, twist slightly and cut with a scissors into 1-inch pieces. If not used at once, wrap in waxed paper. Makes about 4 dozen pieces.

PEACH OR APRICOT LEATHER

The early American candies were homemade. Ingredients were scarce, but good tasting candies were made from sweet supplies on hand. This recipe called for "leather" is an example. It is now being put up for mass consumption and can be bought at candy stores across the country.

1 lb. dried apricots or peaches   **Water**
1 c. sugar

Wash peaches or apricots and soak in water just to cover overnight. Add additional water; boil until fruit is tender. Drain. Run through the food chopper, mix with sugar, and return to the heat to melt the sugar. Spread mixture fairly thin on tin cookie sheets. Place sheets on a table in hot sunshine and cover with a screen frame. Move pans with the sun. When mixture is almost dry, sprinkle lightly with additional sugar. Cut into strips and roll into little rolls. Then roll in sugar and enjoy.

HOT CIDER TODDY.....page 26

Index

Beverages

Hot Cider Toddy..26
Irish Lemonade...70
Mulled Cider..84
Mulled Wine...31
Red Wine Punch...63
Sangaree..49
Southern Spiced Tea..56
Switchel or Haying Water...76
Wassail Bowl..41

Breads

Green Onion Bread...23
Hot Mustard Bread...74
Irish Soda Bread..16
Louisiana Honey Bread..54
Molasses Graham Bread..82
Peanut Bread...29
Prune Bread...60
Spoon Bread..46

Dumplings and Pastry

Crackling Bread...87
Egg Dumplings...59
English Puff Pastry..35
Irish Drop Scones...68
Pot Likker Dumplings..86

Main Dishes

Boiled Irish Ham..65
Boova Shenkel (Boy's Legs)..72
Brunswick Stew...24
Burgoo...15
Calalou..51
Chicken Mold with Almonds..43
Dutch Pork Pie..78
Oregon Beef Fruit Stew..58
Spiced Fish Stew...28
Steak and Kidney Pie..34

Vegetables

Baked Potato and Turnip Puff...53
Baked Stuffed Potatoes...59
Carrot Mold..44
Creamed Cabbage..66
Colcannon...67
Cut (Schnitzel) Beans..74
Green Beans with Mushrooms...45
Green Peas with Mint...37
Mashed Potatoes...36
Pickled Eggs and Red Beets..74
Potato Filling..80
Red Cabbage with Apples..81
Skillet Eggplant and Corn..52

Sauces and Spreads

Cinnamon-Cider Sauce...26
Citrus Rind Marmalade..17
Fresh Churned Butter...20
Hot Lemon and Vanilla Sauce...19
Wine Sauce...31

Desserts

Amish Cake Pie...83
Boiled Custard..39
Chesse Pie..47
Cloth Pudding..18
Creole Fritters..55
Irish Coffee Pudding...69
Marzipan Fruits...40
Miracle Meringue Cake...61
Molasses Taffy..90
Peach or Apricot Leather...91
Pie Crust Pastry..48
Shaker Lemon Pie...75
Stack Cake...88
Steamed Carrot Pudding..30
Steamed Cider Pudding..25
Trifle..38
Windfall Applesauce..89

For a brochure describing other **eberly press** books, please write to:

eberly press

1004 Michigan Ave.

East Lansing, MI 48823